THE EL PASO CHILE COMPANY

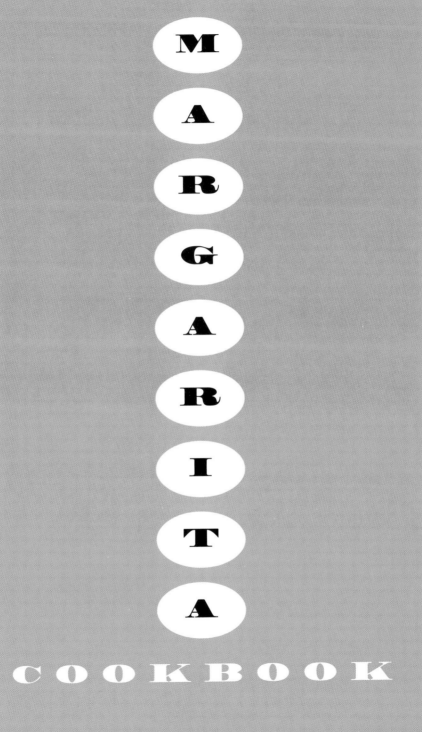

M A R G A R I T A

COOKBOOK

ALSO BY W. PARK KERR

The El Paso Chile Company's Texas Border Cookbook

The El Paso Chile Company's Burning Desires

The El Paso Chile Company's Sizzlin' Suppers

The El Paso Chile Company

Chiles

Tortillas

Beans

THE EL PASO CHILE COMPANY

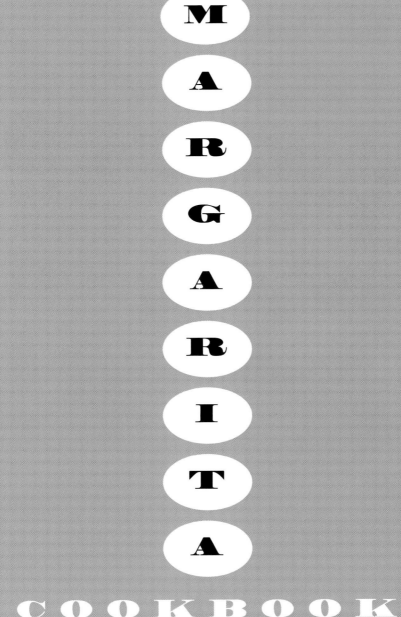

MARGARITA

COOKBOOK

W. PARK KERR

PHOTOGRAPHS BY DUANE WINFIELD

WILLIAM MORROW AND COMPANY, INC.   NEW YORK

Library of Congress Cataloging-in-Publication Data

Kerr, W. Park.

The El Paso Chile Company margarita cookbook / W. Park Kerr;
photographs by Duane Winfield—1st ed.
p.   cm.
Includes index.
ISBN 0-688-16826-4
1. Cocktails.   I. El Paso Chile Company   II. Title.
TX951.K35   1999
641.8'74—dc21   98–55732
                                                   CIP

Printed in Singapore

First Edition

7 8 9 10

BOOK DESIGN BY ELIZABETH VAN ITALLIE

CONTENTS

ACKNOWLEDGMENTS

I'd like to thank the excellent team who worked on shaking up this spirited book. **Muchos Gracias** to Michael McLaughlin for collaborating with me and mixing up all our favorite ingredients (TEQUILA!!!) for this frisky concoction; Justin Schwartz, my editor at Morrow, with one hell of a sense of humor and a delicious vision for the unbelievable creative team he assembled; Duane Winfield—his photographs are brilliant, clear, and genius; Robyn Glazer, the flea market queen, who can spy the perfect thirty-five-cent glass a mile away; Kevin Crafts, the food stylist/engineer, who can transform a lime into a monumental expression of the culinary arts; Elizabeth Van Itallie, for her totally inspiring book design. And to the Morrow staff for putting all of the pieces together so artfully and quickly: Ann Cahn, special projects production editor; Karen Lumley, production manager, and Leah Carlson-Stanisic, art manager for the cookbook division. Once again, Thank you!

INTRODUCTION

Margarita is a fabulous dame, a good time in a glass and the best excuse I know of for planting a lime tree in the backyard. If that tree dies (the ones I plant always do), just cut the damned thing down, buy some limes, and drown your sorrows in the liveliest cocktail known to man—Margarita!

Yes, all right, very good drink indeed, you say, but a whole book's worth? To which I say, *"Sí!"* And that's the beauty of the Margarita. So right, so pure, so fundamental is this most festive of cocktails, it can support any number of delicious improvisations and still maintain its **sabor auténtico** (that's "honest flavor" for those who don't speak Texican). I love Margarita, and I'm faithful and true, but she's a drink with many personalities, all of them worth getting to know, and every one of them is included between the covers of this single-minded book.

Tequila, lime, a little salt—these are the basics. Beyond this power trio (the same one, you'll notice, that makes up the macho ritual of hammering back a jolt of tequila in a single, burning gulp), there are any number of ways to go, each of them leading to one aspect or another of the fascinating Margarita, all them far more civilized than the expression "cactus juice" would lead you to believe. Elegant, blue, basic, up, frosty, on the rocks, or ready for a crowd—this dame is a drink for all seasons, all occasions, and every one of them better for having Margarita on hand.

There's more. At Margarita's heart is tequila, the brash and fiery soul of Mexico. With ice, limes, tequila, and lots of bar glasses on hand, though, I just had to get beyond Margarita, and so this book also offers up tequila cocktails of all kinds—classic, newly invented, or merely tweaked to a new level of existence by the magic of this potent South-of-the-border elixir. If for some loco reason you're not a fan of the Margarita, you'll still find plenty to like and drink in this little but lively book.

There's more still. Margarita even lends her flavor profile to a *cantina* collection of salsas, snacks, tapas-like nibbles, and desserts. Some of these **bocaditos** (little mouthfuls) employ only tequila and lime, while others get a touch of orange liqueur for the complete Margarita makeover. As you feel fabulously transformed by a Margarita or two, so do these sweet and savory snacks.

I don't know who invented the Margarita (although my father says he does; see page 22), and the "when" is suspect as well. Tequila wasn't all that common North of the border until the late 1940s, and even then, travelers to interior Mexico complained that getting anything other than a shot of the stuff was nearly impossible. The Sidecar, a much older drink, consists of brandy, Triple Sec, and lemon juice—a terrific formula just made for tinkering. My own personal theory is that when tequila finally became available, some enterprising bartender at some happening joint somewhere between Houston and Tijuana recognized the Sidecar as a good place to try out that crazy new liquor from Mexico and so made the switch. The really brilliant touch was dusting the rim of the glass with salt, recalling the primitive but effective ritual of Los Tres Amigos (see page 46) while slyly reinforcing its metamorphosis into something graceful and celebratory. Since whoever shook that first shaker of Margs deserves a medal (and a fat pension from the tequila industry), it's regrettable that the moment was not more fully recorded. What can any of us do to properly honor the creator of the Margarita except to order up another round and toast to his— and our—good health? **¡Salud!**

SHOPPING FOR TEQUILA

Remember that, especially with better-quality tequilas, the various makers have distinctive styles. As no two good scotches are alike, so, too, are there big differences among tequilas. While tequila is strictly regulated by the Mexican government, this doesn't mean there aren't cheap, rough tequilas (we all know there are!). It does mean there are some standardized words and phrases that help determine quality: Read the label. Understanding the following terms found there will help you decipher the quality and general flavor profile of the tequila in question, though experimentation (a pleasant process) is the only way to decide which brand or brands most suit your palate.

TEQUILA BLANCO (WHITE) OR PLATA (SILVER)

Not aged, this freshly distilled product can be as rough as kerosene or fiery sweet and a tequila-lover's delight. The best of these will also bear on their labels the phrase "100 percent blue agave." This means that 100 percent of the tequila's sugars come from the blue agave plant (**Agave tequilana "Weber"**), a standard of flavor that cannot be met by tequilas sugared in more ordinary (and less expensive) ways. It also means that the tequila was bottled at its origin in Mexico, unlike cheaper liquors that come into the United States in tanker cars and are bottled here.

A 100 percent blue agave **blanco** or **plata** tequila sings with the flavor of both the plant and the soil where it was grown. It's fine for drinking straight in shots or for using in cocktails where you want a distinctive tequila taste.

TEQUILA "JOVAN ABOCADO" ("YOUNG AND SMOOTH"): GOLD TEQUILA

Though it appears to have been aged, it has not. By Mexican law gold tequila is actually defined as silver tequila to which caramel or other coloring and flavoring has been added. The additions typically mellow and smooth the flavor of the tequila. Gold tequila is well suited for shots and shooters, or for those a little wary of the bigger flavors of white or silver tequila.

TEQUILA "REPOSADO": "RESTED" TEQUILA

This distinctively delicious and mellow tequila has been aged for at least two months (or up to one year) in oak tanks or barrels. In addition, most **reposado** tequilas are made from 100 percent blue agave. As with other aged spirits (wine, bourbon, Cognac), the time the tequila spends in wood smoothes and improves it, adding such flavor nuances as vanilla and honey. The color change that results from the aging varies from pale to medium gold (and coloring may be added as well), and for many drinkers **reposado** tequila is what gold tequila could or should be but isn't. This tequila can be sipped neat (shots would be an insult) or used in Cadillac-quality Margaritas.

TEQUILA "AÑEJO" AND "MUY AÑEJO": AGED TEQUILAS

These ultimate tequilas are aged for at least one year and up to four in barrels sealed by the government. Nearly all **añejo** tequilas are made from 100 percent blue agave. They are label-dated (if tequilas from more than one year are blended, the bottle will be dated with the most recent year); colorings and flavorings are permitted and, as with all tequilas, purified water is added as necessary to adjust the proof. Connoisseurs look for **añejo** tequilas in which the flavor of the original tequila and that of the wood remain in some balance. Out-of-kilter **añejos** can taste like nothing but wood, which misses the point for those, like me, who love tequila for its own sake.

HOW TEQUILA
IS MADE

Tequila is produced from the huge central cores (called **piñas**, for their resemblance to pineapples) of the blue agave plant. Though spiky, it's a member of the lily family and not a cactus at all. The blue agave is farmed for tequila production in a small area of Mexico that is strictly delineated by law. When ripe, the **piñas**, which can weigh up to one hundred pounds, are harvested by machete-wielding field veterans called **mescaleros**. (Harvesting kills the plants, which can be ten or more years old.) The **piñas** are then baked, which converts their starches to sugar. Different distilleries use methods either rustic (adobe ovens) or high-tech (autoclaves), but the result is the same—the **piñas** emerge transformed, looking and tasting, as tequila expert Lucinda Hutson puts it, like "cooked sweet potatoes drenched in honey."

The baked **piñas** are coarsely shredded and, along with their syrup, left to ferment for about a week. The beer-like mixture that results is then double-distilled, removing impurities (some toxic) and off flavors and raising its proof. The potent liquor is now ready to be bottled and drunk as white or silver tequila, or further transformed by aging into another type of tequila.

WHERE'S THE WORM?

The tequila novice may be expecting to see a worm at the bottom of his bottle of plata. Not so! Worms are found in mezcal, another agave-based distilled Mexican liquor. The worms are actually the larvae of an insect that lives in the agave and thus serve as a sign of authenticity, not to mention a topic of conversation. Unlike tequila, mezcal is produced without government regulation, in various regions of Mexico, and in a variety of local styles, the differences at least partially due to the type of agave used. Tequila is, in fact, a regional mezcal that, through popularity, regulation, and promotion, has risen to prominence.

Most of the mezcal found in this country comes from Oaxaca and can be pleasant but unremarkable. For a real treat, though, visit Oaxaca itself, and shop for artisanal, or small-batch, mezcals, sold, along with other tourist souvenirs, in small stores called *tiendas*. Sample before buying if possible, since quality varies enormously. Usually drunk as shots or oyster shooters, *mezcal* is worth seeking out. The worm is usually presented to the honored guest; after a number of shots of fiery *mezcal*, eating a small *mezcal*-marinated critter will probably seem a perfectly logical thing to do.

Blue Margarita

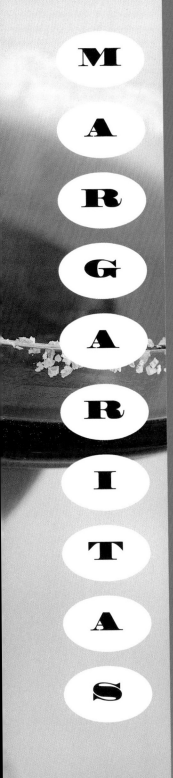

M A R G A R I T A S

THE KENTUCKY CLUB MARGARITA

MAKES 1 COCKTAIL

In the beginning, this was it—El Original, Número Uno—created, according to my father, at the Kentucky Club, just across the border from El Paso in wild and wooly Juarez, Mexico, in the early forties (At last count twenty-seven other sites throughout the Western Hemisphere were also claiming to be "The Home of the Margarita," but I learned a long time ago not to argue with Dad.) This drink is strong and relatively tart.

> 1 lime wedge
> Kosher salt on a small plate
> 1 1/2 ounces tequila
> 1 ounce fresh lime juice, preferably from Mexican limes
> 1/2 ounce orange liqueur, such as Controy Licor de
>   Naranjas or Triple Sec

Run the lime wedge around the rim of a highball glass. Dip the moistened rim in the salt. Set the lime wedge and glass aside.

In a shaker half-filled with ice cubes, combine the tequila, lime juice, and orange liqueur. Shake like hell. Fill the prepared glass with fresh ice cubes. Strain the contents of the shaker into the glass. Squeeze the lime wedge into the cocktail, drop the wedge into the glass, and serve immediately.

TEQUILA TIP In Mexico, Margaritas are frequently made with Controy Licor de Naranjas, a Cointreau-inspired (OK, knocked-off) orange liqueur that comes in bright green glass bottles. It's very sweet (which is why bartenders cut back on it) but very cheap, which is why I always bring back lots from a trip across the border. It's especially useful for a party-sized batch of Frozen Margaritas (page 29) or my Trailer Park Punch (page 30).

THREE-CITRUS
SUNRISE MARGARITA

MAKES 1 COCKTAIL

Subtle adjustments to the classic formula make for great big changes in this Margarita variation. The three citrus juices come through loud and clear, while the dollop of Chambord at the heart of the cocktail supplies the hue of the rising sun. I like this "up" (but then I like most Margaritas that way), but it's good on the rocks too.

> 1 lime wedge
> Kosher salt on a small plate
> 1 1/2 ounces tequila
> 1 ounce Triple Sec
> 1/2 ounce fresh lime juice
> 1/2 ounce fresh orange juice
> 1/2 ounce fresh grapefruit juice
> 1 teaspoon Chambord (black raspberry liqueur)

Run the lime wedge around the rim of a stemmed cocktail glass. Dip the moistened rim in the salt. Set the lime wedge and glass aside.

In a cocktail shaker half-filled with ice cubes, combine the tequila, Triple Sec, lime juice, orange juice, and grapefruit juice. Shake well, then strain into the prepared glass. Squeeze the lime wedge into the cocktail and discard. Carefully add the Chambord to the center of the cocktail, letting it sink to the bottom of the glass without blending it into the rest of the drink. Serve immediately.

MARGARITA 101

Here, fine-tuned for those folks who find the authentic Mexican-style Margarita (as prepared at the Kentucky Club) too tart, is the purely perfect introductory version, neatly and sweetly balanced. If you try only one Margarita recipe in your lifetime, make it this one.

> 1 lime wedge
> Kosher salt on a small plate
> 1 ½ ounces tequila
> 1 ounce orange liqueur, such as Controy Licor de Naranjas
> or Triple Sec
> 1 ounce fresh lime juice

Run the lime wedge around the rim of a highball glass. Dip the moistened rim in the salt. Set the lime wedge and glass aside.

In a shaker half-filled with ice cubes, combine the tequila, Triple Sec, and lime juice. Shake well. Fill the prepared glass with fresh ice. Strain the cocktail into the glass. Squeeze the lime wedge into the Margarita, drop the wedge into the glass, and serve immediately.

TEQUILA TIP Intensely flavorful and fragrant, the small, yellow-skinned Mexican lime (*limone*) is the same variety known in Florida as the Key lime. Those grown in Mexico were once prohibited entry into this country, but now they can be brought back over the border and do make a superior Margarita. On the other hand, large, dark green Persian limes, the ones commonly found at the supermarket, work just fine too.

MARGARITA 1-TO-1-TO-1

This elegant but potent drink will remind you of the classic Gimlet—it's a Margarita for grown-ups. Built from equal parts tequila, Cointreau, and lime juice, it's based on a formula that's easy to measure and easy to remember—although if you're having memory problems, a cup of coffee might be the wiser choice.

> 1 lime wedge
> Kosher salt on a small plate
> 1 ounce tequila
> 1 ounce Cointreau or other premium orange liqueur
> 1 ounce fresh lime juice

Run the lime wedge around the rim of a stemmed cocktail glass. Dip the moistened rim in the salt. Set the lime wedge and glass aside.

In a cocktail shaker half-filled with ice cubes, combine the tequila, Cointreau, and lime juice. Shake well, then strain into the prepared glass. Squeeze the lime wedge into the cocktail and discard. Serve immediately.

TEQUILA TIP The best cocktail jigger is the double-headed hourglass-shaped kind, with one side measuring one ounce, the other side one and one half. If you don't have a jigger, you can use less-elegant measuring spoons; just do your mixing out of sight in the kitchen. One ounce is 2 tablespoons; one and one half are 3 tablespoons, and so on.

MELON MARGARITA

Margaritas without some kind of orange liqueur may seem like heresy, but here is one version in which a substitution pays dividends. Midori, the Japanese green melon liqueur, adds color and unique flavor to a Margarita that is sure to win converts. I garnish these with balls of cantaloupe that have been skewered onto cocktail picks and then frozen.

> 1 lime wedge
> Kosher salt on a small plate
> 1½ ounces tequila
> 1 ounce Midori
> 1 ounce fresh lime juice
> Melon balls frozen on a cocktail pick as garnish, optional

Run the lime wedge around the rim of a large stemmed glass. Dip the moistened rim in the salt. Set aside.

In a cocktail shaker half-filled with ice, combine the tequila, Midori, and lime juice. Shake well, then strain into the prepared glass. Garnish with the melon ball skewer, if desired, and serve immediately.

TEQUILA TIP When a crowd's on the way, Margarita glasses can be salted and set aside well in advance. Once the lime juice dries, the salt will stay firmly in place, and you can use those last minutes before the doorbell rings to vacuum the living room, marinate the steaks, or quietly enjoy a Margarita all to yourself.

TEQUILA [...] zen Strawberry
Margaritas, replac[...] with about 3 cups
chopped fresh or p[...] rozen berries. Blend
as directed, and gar[...] argarita with a single,
perfect berry.

MY FROSTY FROZEN MARGARITAS

MAKES 12 LARGE COCKTAILS

In summer, the daytime temperature in El Paso can go for weeks without dropping below 100 degrees, and an icy Marg is just the thing to provide relief. Straight from the blender, these are slushy but pourable; stored in a covered container in the freezer overnight, they become firmer, almost granita-like, and can be served in stemmed glasses, garnished with fresh berries, as a breathtakingly cold dessert.

> 3 limes, quartered
> Kosher salt on a small plate
> One 6-ounce container frozen limeade concentrate, thawed
> 1½ cups tequila
> ¾ cup Controy Licor de Naranjas or other orange liqueur
> ¼ cup fresh lime juice
> About 4 trays ice cubes
> One 6-ounce container frozen pineapple juice concentrate, thawed

Run one of the lime wedges around the rim of a stemmed cocktail glass. Dip the moistened rim in the salt and set the glass aside. Repeat with eleven more glasses.

In a blender, combine the limeade concentrate, half the tequila, half the orange liqueur, and half the lime juice. Fill the blender almost to the top with ice cubes, cover, and blend on high speed until thick and slushy. Transfer to a decorative pitcher. Repeat with the remaining tequila, orange liqueur, and lime juice, the pineapple juice concentrate, and more ice. Transfer to the pitcher and stir to blend. The Margaritas can be served immediately or stored, covered, in the refrigerator for several hours.

To serve, pour (or spoon) into the prepared glasses. Squeeze a wedge of lime into each drink and serve immediately.

TRAILER PARK PUNCH

MAKES 30 COCKTAILS

Sometimes everyone you know piles into a van and heads
over to your place for a good time. With a mob on the way,
a big **ponche** (punch) of some kind is just the ticket. This one
goes together quickly and tastes great even when made with
inexpensive tequila. It starts out a little stronger than you may
want, but when the ice that keeps it cold begins to melt, the
drinks come out just right. See the tip on page 27 about
salting glasses in advance.

> Two 12-ounce containers frozen limeade concentrate,
>   thawed
> 3 cups tequila
> 3 cups water
> 2 cups orange liquor, such as Triple Sec
> 1 cup fresh lime juice
> Thinly sliced lemons, limes, or oranges as garnish,
>   optional

Combine all the ingredients except the garnish in a container and
chill well (preferably overnight).

To serve, transfer to a punch bowl. Add 2 medium blocks of ice
(see below). Ladle the punch into glasses and float the citrus
slices in the drinks, if desired.

TEQUILA TIP Use an ice ring if you must
(freeze it in a savarin mold or Bundt pan), but simple
blocks of ice (I use 2-pint plastic food storage contain-
ers) work just fine.

BLUE
MARGARITA

MAKES 1 COCKTAIL

Why make a Margarita blue? Well, because the neon color is festive and unexpected, for one thing. Also, despite the artificial coloring it takes to turn the Curaçao blue, some brands, such as Bols, are among the most richly flavorful orange liqueurs available. Use Bols and your Margarita will taste as unexpectedly delicious as it looks.

> 1 lime wedge
> Kosher salt on a small plate
> 1 ½ ounces tequila
> 1 ½ ounces fresh lime juice
> 1 ounce blue Curaçao, preferably Bols brand

Run the lime wedge around the rim of a stemmed cocktail glass. Dip the moistened rim in the salt. Set the lime wedge and glass aside.

In a cocktail shaker half-filled with ice cubes, combine the tequila, lime juice, and Curaçao. Shake well, then strain into the prepared glass. Squeeze the lime wedge into the cocktail, drop the wedge into the glass, and serve immediately.

See photo on page 20.

SANTA FE
SILVER SATIN

MAKES 1 COCKTAIL

In the style of the seventy-five or so Margaritas on the menu at Maria's New Mexico Kitchen, a popular Santa Fe restaurant, is this smooth concoction. Maria's owner, Al Lucero, finds lemons more consistent in quality year-round than limes and so substitutes their juice in his unconventional cocktails, frequently made with 100 percent blue agave tequila and a premium orange liqueur. They're smooth as satin, they break the rules, and they work for me!

> 1 lime wedge
> Kosher salt on a small plate
> 1¼ ounces premium silver tequila, preferably 100 percent
>   blue agave
> 1 ounce Grand Marnier
> 1 ounce fresh lemon juice

Run the lime wedge around the rim of an old-fashioned glass. Dip the moistened rim in the salt. Set the lime wedge and glass aside.

In a shaker half-filled with ice cubes, combine the tequila, Grand Marnier, and lemon juice. Shake well. Fill the prepared glass with fresh ice. Strain the cocktail into the glass. Squeeze the lime wedge into the Margarita, drop the wedge into the glass, and serve immediately.

TEQUILA TIP Standard bar-glass lingo for a short rocks glass is an "old-fashioned," while the conical stemmed Martini or Margarita glass is a "cocktail." If ever there were a drink for which the rules were made to be broken, however, it's the Margarita. At Maria's, for example, Margaritas on the rocks are served in hurricane-type glasses. I often use canning jars for regular Margaritas on the rocks or for Rio Grande Lemonade (page 56), and I serve my famous frozen Margs in a wacky set of cocktail glasses whose stems are actually green glass saguaro cacti.

MANGO MARGARITA
À LA MODE

MAKES 1 COCKTAIL

A golden mango Margarita is a very fine thing indeed though it's even better when a small scoop of berry sorbet is set afloat in it. If I have Quick Raspberry Margarita Sorbet (page 109) on hand, I use it, but the tequila-free Häagen-Dazs works just fine too. (Equally appropriate though not as colorful are mango and Margarita sorbets, also from Häagen-Dazs.) This is one of the few Margaritas that is better without salt.

> 2 ounces tequila
> 1 ounce Grand Marnier or other orange liqueur
> 1 ounce fresh lime juice
> 2 tablespoons pureed ripe mango
> ½ ounce mango nectar, optional
> 1 small ball raspberry or strawberry sorbet

In a cocktail shaker half-filled with ice cubes, combine the tequila, Grand Marnier, lime juice, and mango puree. Shake well, then strain into a stemmed cocktail glass. Add the mango nectar, if desired. Float the ball of sorbet in the Margarita and serve immediately.

TEQUILA TIP Mangoes are increasingly common, but if whole mangoes are not available, look for refrigerated jarred mangoes in the produce section. Drain the sweet syrup and rinse the pieces before pureeing in a food processor or blender.

PINEAPPLE TEQUILA

MAKES 3/4 LITER

My kitchen is never without a big batch of this golden, fruity
tequila working away. It makes fine Pineapple Margaritas
(page 38), it's essential in a frosty Tequila Colada (page 66),
and when the tequila is gone, any remaining softened fruit can
be chopped, warmed in butter with additional brown sugar, and
used to top a big bowl of macadamia brittle ice cream.

> One 750-ml bottle good-quality tequila, preferably gold
> 1 very ripe and juicy large pineapple, trimmed, peeled,
>   quartered, cored, and cut into 2-inch chunks
> 1 vanilla bean, split lengthwise
> 2 tablespoons packed light brown sugar

In a medium container (a jar with a lid works well), combine the
tequila, pineapple, vanilla bean, and sugar. Cover and let stand at
room temperature, stirring once a day, for 1 week before using.
Refrigerate indefinitely for long-term storage.

PINEAPPLE
MARGARITAS

These frothy (not actually frozen) Margaritas, made with my pineapple-infused tequila, will have your happy mouth doing the hula. Serve them to kick off your next backyard luau.

> 4 lime wedges
> Kosher salt on a small plate
> 2 cups ice cubes
> 3 ounces Pineapple Tequila (page 36)
> 4 chunks pineapple from Pineapple Tequila
> 1/3 cup fresh lime juice
> 2 ounces Triple Sec

Run a lime wedge around the rim of a large stemmed cocktail glass. Dip the moistened rim in the salt. Set the lime wedge and glass aside. Repeat with the remaining wedge and 3 more glasses.

In a blender jar, combine the ice, tequila, pineapple, lime juice, and Triple Sec. Blend on high speed until smooth and frothy. Divide the Margaritas among the prepared glasses. Squeeze a lime wedge into each glass, drop the wedge into the glass, and serve immediately.

TEQUILA TIP As cocktails have grown in popularity, so, too, has their size increased. Bar glasses the size of aquariums are now used to serve Martinis and Margaritas and imbibers are forced to slug them down in unseemly haste in order to enjoy them icy-cold, or drink them lukewarm, the result of sipping them sensibly. How much you drink is up to you, but when it comes to cocktails, smaller drinks, refreshed more often and savored chilled, are the only way to go.

PASSION-PEACH MARGARITA

MAKES 1 COCKTAIL

Alizé is a passion-fruit-juice-and-Cognac liqueur that imparts a flavor of faraway places to this fresh peach Margarita. When I'm really feeling festive, I garnish this with a single small, perfect orchid.

> 1 lime wedge
> Kosher salt on a small plate
> 1 ½ ounces tequila
> 3 tablespoons pureed ripe peach
> 1 ounce Alizé
> ½ teaspoon Cointreau
> 1 small orchid, as garnish, optional

Run the lime wedge around the rim of a stemmed cocktail glass. Dip the moistened rim in the salt. Set the glass aside.

In a cocktail shaker half-filled with ice cubes, combine the tequila, peach puree, Alizé, and Cointreau. Shake well, then strain into the prepared glass. Garnish with the orchid, if desired.

TRIPLE CITRUS TEQUILA

MAKES 3/4 LITER

Tequila and citrus are natural amigos, so why not infuse a whole bottle of the powerful stuff with the combined flavors of orange, lemon, and lime? The result works great in a Margarita, but it makes even more sense in my Texatini (page 63) or in the Frozen Watermelon Margaritas (recipe follows). Or enjoy an icy shot straight from the freezer.

> One 750-ml bottle good-quality silver tequila
> Zest (colored peel) of 1 large orange, removed in 1 long thin strip with a peeler
> Zest of 2 large lemons, removed in long thin strips
> Zest of 2 large limes, removed in a long thin strips

Pour out and reserve about ½ cup of the tequila. Add the citrus zests to the tequila (a chopstick helps push them down in). Return the reserved tequila to the bottle, cap the bottle, and let the tequila stand, agitating the bottle occasionally, for 48 hours before using. Freeze for long-term storage.

FROZEN WATERMELON MARGARITAS

MAKES 4 COCKTAILS

For these refreshing ruby-colored cocktails, I freeze chunks of melon (select a dead-ripe, juicy, flavorful one). Blended with the melon as the only chilling agent, the drinks are not diluted, and the delicate flavor of the fruit comes though. Gold watermelon can be substituted.

> 4 cups 1-inch chunks seedless watermelon
> 4 lime wedges
> Kosher salt on a small plate
> ¾ cup Triple Citrus Tequila (page 40) or any good-quality
>   tequila
> ½ cup Triple Sec
> ⅓ cup fresh lime juice

Place the melon chunks in a plastic bag, and freeze until solid.

Run a lime wedge around the rim of a large stemmed cocktail glass. Dip the moistened rim in the salt. Set the lime wedge and glass aside. Repeat with the remaining wedges and 3 more glasses.

Transfer about three fourths of the melon chunks, separating them, to a blender jar. Add the tequila, Triple Sec, and lime juice and blend until fairly smooth. Add the remaining melon and blend until smooth. Divide the cocktail mixture among the prepared glasses. Squeeze a lime wedge into each cocktail, drop the wedge into the glass, and serve immediately.

TEQUILA TIP For an extra touch of color and flavor, mix 2 teaspoons finely minced lime zest (colored peel) into the salt before rimming the glass.

T E Q U I L A

STRAIGHT

LOS TRES AMIGOS

SERVES 1

This is more method than recipe, but the salt-lime-and-shot ritual is an important part of the tequila mystique, and it's worth knowing how to do it right. First, it's your drink and you can do what you want, in the order you want to. Nevertheless, there is a plan behind the madness. In Mexico, the trio of salt, tequila, and lime (and that is the correct order) is called **los tres amigos** (the three friends), and the goal is to let the tequila—which unless one of the top premium types is fairly rough—slip down as easily as possible. You may want to sip your forty-dollars-a-bottle **reposado** tequila without adornment (and you should), but when it's just standard silver **cantina** tequila, salt before and lime after are essential. Lick the junction of your thumb and fore-finger. Salt the wet spot. In one smooth motion, lick the salt, then, using the salted hand, grab and gulp the shot of tequila, grab a wedge of lime, and bite it, squeezing juice into your mouth. Make a face now, if you think that will help. That's it— that's tequila **cruda**, rough and ready but a hell of a lot of fun, as long as you don't repeat the process too many times.

LUCINDA HUTSON'S JALISCO SANGRITA

MAKES ABOUT 2¼ CUPS (TO CHASE 7 TO 8 SHOTS)

My friend Lucinda Hutson knows more about tequila than almost anyone, and her recipe for sangrita, the fiery citrus-chile blend that is Mexico's favorite tequila chaser, is the best. To savor sangrita as it is in Jalisco, where they know their tequila, serve shots of best-quality tequila and chase them with equal-sized shots of chilled sangrita. It may seem like a large quantity, but don't worry, the sangrita will keep for a week or so. Use any flavorful (not just hot) hot sauce you like, and adjust the amount to your taste.

> 2 cups fresh orange juice
> ¼ cup hot sauce, such as Hellfire & Damnation
> 1 ounce fresh lime juice
> ½ ounce grenadine
> ¼ teaspoon salt

In a jar or other covered container, combine all the ingredients. Cover and chill overnight before using.

TEQUILA TIP Though the intense tequila-sangrita chaser experience is pretty much perfect, Lucinda quite rightly points out that the two can also be combined for a tasty cocktail. For her Maria Sangrita, in a tall glass of ice, combine ½ cup sangrita, 1½ ounces best-quality tequila, the juice of ½ lime, ½ teaspoon grated onion, and salt and freshly ground black pepper to taste. Stir well. If you use a scallion brush as garnish, as Lucinda suggests, be sure to wear your safety goggles!

Tequila Cosmopolitan

c o

CKTAILS

CLASSIC AND NUEVO

TEQUILA SUNRISE

This tall, mellow juice-and-tequila classic seems particularly appropriate at brunch, but then it's great at the end of the day as well—called, perhaps, a Tequila Sunset? Grenadine, an artificially colored red syrup, traditionally provides the ruby glow at the bottom of the glass, but I prefer to use the black raspberry liqueur Chambord.

> 1/2 cup fresh orange juice
> 2 ounces tequila
> 1/2 ounce Chambord
> Splash of club soda, optional
> 1 lime wedge

Fill a highball glass about three-quarters full of ice. Add the juice and tequila and stir to blend. Add the Chambord, letting it sink to the bottom of the glass. Top the cocktail with club soda, if desired. Squeeze the lime wedge into the drink, drop the wedge into the glass, and serve immediately.

TEQUILA WALLBANGER

MAKES 1 COCKTAIL

Replacing the vodka with tequila in the classic Harvey Wallbanger turns it into a Freddy Fudpucker (or so the bar guides say). Call it what you will (and I recommend you call it anything but that!), it's a smooth but lively way to get your tequila ration, and a nice introduction to the sweetly herbal pleasures of golden Galliano.

> 2 ounces tequila
> ½ cup plus 2 tablespoons fresh orange juice
> ½ ounce Galliano

In a tall glass, stir together the tequila and orange juice. Fill the glass with ice cubes. Float the Galliano atop the cocktail and serve immediately.

TEQUILA TIP This general plan can also be followed using any of your favorite orange liqueurs in place of the Galliano. And when I can find it, either tangerine juice (add a squeeze of lime) or blood orange juice makes a nice substitute for the plain OJ.

SALTY CHIHUAHUA

MAKES 1 COCKTAIL

A tequila take on the very refreshing Salty Dog, this drink is named in honor of my son's pet, Maximillian. Those who like things sweeter may prefer this made with pink or even ruby grapefruit juice; it's then called a Pink Chihuahua. Under either title, it's a great brunch drink that's also pretty damned good when the cocktail hour rolls around.

> 1 lime wedge
> Kosher salt on a small plate
> 2 ounces tequila
> 1/3 to 1/2 cup fresh grapefruit juice

Run the lime wedge around the rim of a highball glass. Set the lime wedge aside. Dip the moistened rim in the salt. Fill the glass about three-quarters full of ice. Add the tequila and top with grapefruit juice to taste. Stir to blend. Squeeze the lime wedge into the drink, drop the wedge into the glass, and serve immediately.

TEQUILA TIP For a flavor twist (especially if your grapefruit juice is very tart), rim the glass with a mixture of kosher salt and sugar.

RIO GRANDE
LEMONADE

MAKES 6 SERVINGS

Less potent than a Margarita and very refreshing, this tangy,
tasty cooler is always on hand when I light the grill and hungry—
and thirsty—guests gather in the backyard. Lime juice can
replace some of the lemon juice, if you like, and sprigs of mint,
picked fresh from the garden, make a fine garnish.

> 2 1/2 cups fresh lemon juice, strained
> 2 cups water
> About 1 2/3 cups sugar
> 3/4 cup tequila

In a nonreactive container, such as a pitcher or jar, stir together
the lemon juice, water, 1 1/4 cups of the sugar, and the tequila.
Cover and refrigerate until very cold, preferably overnight.

Taste the lemonade and add more sugar to taste. Stir to
completely dissolve. Serve the lemonade over lots of ice in 1-pint
canning jars or beer mugs.

HOMEMADE SWEET-AND-SOUR DRINK BASE

Makes about 4 cups

Most commercial sweet-and-sours have all the citrusy freshness of lemon furniture polish. To avoid cocktails that taste like Pledge, I make my own drink base. It goes together in a few minutes (especially if I can find a volunteer to squeeze the limes and lemons), keeps well in the refrigerator, and improves any number of cocktail hours. It can also be enjoyed as is, without alcohol, served over ice with a splash of soda.

> 2 cups water
> 1 cup sugar
> ½ cup fresh lime juice
> ½ cup fresh lemon juice

In a small heavy saucepan, combine the water and sugar. Set over low heat and stir until the sugar dissolves. Transfer to a jar with a lid. Cool to room temperature, then stir in the lime and lemon juices, cover, and refrigerate until chilled before using. The drink base will keep for up to 1 week in the regfrigerator, or it can be frozen for up to 1 month.

PINK LIMEADE

MAKES 1 COCKTAIL

Tall, pale pink, and cooling, this quaff is very nice at the end of a long, thirsty day. You can make it with purchased sweet-and-sour mix if time is tight, but my homemade version that follows is infinitely fresher- and better-tasting.

> 3 ounces Homemade Sweet-and-Sour Drink Base
> (page 57)
> 2 ounces tequila
> 1 1/2 ounces cranberry juice cocktail
> 1/2 ounce fresh lime juice
> 1 lime wedge

In a shaker half-filled with ice, combine the sweet-and-sour base, tequila, cranberry juice, and lime juice. Shake well. Fill a highball glass with fresh ice. Strain the cocktail into the glass, squeeze the lime wedge into the drink, and drop the wedge into the glass. Serve immediately.

HOT 'N' COLD CHILE TEQUILA

MAKES ABOUT 1 ½ PINTS

chile-infused tequila is hot stuff, all right, but since
e freezer until syrupy cold, it also soothes the pain
shot (with a chaser of Sangrita—page 47—or just a
piece of lime to chew on) is one very fine way to abolish the
memories of a bad day at the office. For those who can't get
enough jalapeños (my hand is up), this is also great in a Texatini
(page 63), Bloody Maria (page 68), or El Chupacabra (page 70).

> One 750-ml bottle best-quality silver tequila
> 2 jalapeño chiles (1 red and 1 green, if possible),
>   stemmed and quartered lengthwise
> 1 scallion, top and bottom trimmed to fit in the tequila
>   bottle
> 1 serrano chile, stemmed and halved lengthwise
> 1 small dried red chile, such as chile de arból, stemmed,
>   split, and seeded
> 1 large clove garlic, halved lengthwise
> Zest (colored peel) of 1 lime or ½ orange, removed in a
>   long thin strip with a peeler

Pour out and reserve about ½ cup of the tequila. Add the
jalapeños, scallion, serrano, dried chile, garlic, and citrus zest to
the bottle (a chopstick helps push them down). Top off the
bottle with the reserved tequila (drink whatever won't fit into
the bottle).

Let stand at room temperature, shaking the bottle occasionally,
for 48 hours, then store the bottle in the freezer. The tequila will
become thick and syrupy. Serve directly from the freezer.

TEQUILA TIKI

For a good time, shake your tiki! No surprise—I find this tequila cousin of the Mai Tai head and shoulders above the rum-based original. These days appropriately silly paper parasols and other daffy cocktail decorations are easy to find, but for the essential sweet almond syrup called **orgeat** (pronounced or-ZHAH), you'll need to visit a very well stocked specialty liquor store. Don't omit it: When it comes to making a terrific Tiki, it's orgeat or else!

> 2 ounces Triple Citrus Tequila (page 40) or any good-
>   quality gold or silver tequila
> 1 ounce Curaçao or Triple Sec
> 1 ounce fresh lime juice
> 2 teaspoons orgeat (see headnote)
> 1 teaspoon grenadine
> Strips of pineapple, slices of orange, and/or assorted
>   paper or plastic tropical cocktail decorations

In a cocktail shaker half-filled with ice, combine the tequila, Curaçao, lime juice, orgeat, and grenadine. Shake well. Pour the contents of the shaker into a large wide stemmed cocktail glass (the more dramatic, the better). Decorate as desired and serve immediately, preferably with a straw for sipping.

TEXATINI

MAKES 1 COCKTAIL

I'm lucky enough to wear jeans rather than a three-piece suit to work, but at the end of a long day, just like those gray flannel guys on the commuter trains, I crave something in the Martini zone. Since I'm Texas born, I shake up an icy Texatini or two. Infused tequila is a fine option here, but the plain stuff also does the job. Garnish your 'tini with a tequila-marinated olive and serrano chile or a twist of lime peel.

> 2 ounces Triple Citrus Tequila (page 40), Hot 'n' Cold
> Chile Tequila (page 61), or any best-quality gold or
> silver tequila, preferably chilled
> ½ ounce dry vermouth (or to taste), preferably chilled
> 1 olive and 1 serrano chile, preferably from Margarita-
> Marinated Cocktail Olives (page 84), on a cocktail
> pick, or 1 short strip lime zest (colored peel)

Fill a cocktail shaker half-full of ice. Add the tequila and vermouth and shake until very cold. Strain into a stemmed cocktail glass. Add the olive and chile, or twist the lime peel over the drink and then drop it into the glass. Serve immediately.

TEQUILA TIP For the Texatini, or any cocktail that is at its best very strong and very cold, starting with chilled ingredients reduces the amount of dilution from melting ice. The ice should also be "dry"— that is, it should not be wet (no running the ice cube tray under water to release the cubes, for example). You'll know you've done things right if the tequila smokes when you add it to the shaker.

CHIMAYO COCKTAIL

In the fields surrounding the beautiful mountain village of Chimayo, New Mexico, north of Santa Fe, the two principal crops are wonderfully sweet-hot red chiles and tasty apples of many varieties. The two come together with brilliant results at Rancho de Chimayo, a restaurant famed for its red chile–seasoned dishes and for this cider-based cocktail, especially appropriate when there's a nip of fall in the air.

> 3 ounces tequila
> 2 ounces apple cider, preferably fresh and unfiltered
> 1/2 ounce fresh lemon juice
> 1/2 ounce crème de cassis (black currant liqueur)
> 2 thin apple wedges (from a small apple)

In a shaker half-filled with ice, combine the tequila, cider, lemon juice, and cassis. Shake well. Fill two old-fashioned glasses with fresh ice. Strain the cocktail into the glasses, dividing evenly. Garnish each glass with an apple wedge and serve immediately.

TEQUILA COLADA

In a hammock, by a shack, on a beach, under a swaying palm tree, or wherever you happen to sip this tropical treat, you'll automatically be on vacation. My general rule of idyllic getaways applies here (in spirit, anyway): Don't come home until you have to! For a colder, less powerful cocktail, blend rather than shake this drink.

> 1 ½ ounces tequila
> 3 tablespoons well-blended coconut cream
> 1 ounce Curaçao or other orange liqueur
> 1 ounce pineapple juice
> 1 ounce fresh lime juice
> 1 lime wedge
> Toasted, shredded coconut (optional)

In a shaker half-filled with ice, combine the tequila, coconut cream, Curaçao, pineapple juice, and lime juice. Shake well. Pour the contents of the shaker into a large, dramatic stemmed cocktail glass. Squeeze the lime wedge into the cocktail, then discard it. Sprinkle the coconut on top, if desired. Serve immediately.

BLOODY MARIA

MAKES 1 COCKTAIL

In a Bloody Mary, it's the tomato juice and the seasonings that are the stars; in this chunky Southwestern variation of that classic, however, it's the tequila that shines. Since I once nearly put an eye out with a stalk of celery growing from an otherwise delicious Bloody, I skip the produce, but you can feel free to garnish this to your heart's content—with red pepper flakes maybe?

> 1 lime wedge
> Kosher salt on a small plate
> 1/3 cup to 1/2 cup good-quality tomato juice
> 2 ounces tequila
> 1/2 ounce fresh lime juice
> 2 heaping tablespoons salsa or pico de gallo, or to taste
> 1 teaspoon Worcestershire sauce

Run the lime wedge around the rim of a highball glass. Dip the moistened rim in the salt. Set the lime wedge and glass aside.

In a shaker half-filled with ice cubes, combine the tomato juice, tequila, lime juice, salsa, and Worcestershire sauce. Shake well. Pour the cocktail into the glass. Squeeze the lime wedge into the drink, drop the wedge into the glass, and serve immediately.

TEQUILA TIP For an extra touch of flavor and color, add 2 teaspoons medium-hot powdered red chile to the salt before rimming the glasses.

EL CHUPACABRA
(THE VAMPIRE)

<small>MAKES 1 COCKTAIL</small>

Blood-red, subtly spicy, and deeply flavored by the chile puree, this elegant cocktail is only vaguely related to the Bloody Mary. Don't be afraid to serve this at your next Halloween costume party—the touch of garlic will keep the real vampires at bay.

> $1/2$ cup good-quality tomato juice
>
> $1 1/2$ ounces tequila
>
> 1 tablespoon frozen medium-hot red chile puree, thawed, or 2 tablespoons salsa or pico de gallo
>
> $1/2$ ounce fresh lime juice
>
> $1/8$ teaspoon garlic powder
>
> $1/8$ teaspoon salt

In a shaker half-filled with ice cubes, combine the tomato juice, tequila, chile puree, lime juice, garlic powder, and salt. Shake well. Pour into a glass and serve immediately.

BAJA BEACH BUM

If I can't actually become a beach bum in Mexico, I can at least drink one of these spicy potions come cocktail hour. Make it with good hot but thin salsa, like a picante sauce, and set out a bowl of oyster crackers to munch on.

1/2 cup V-8 juice, Clamato juice, or good-quality plain tomato juice

2 1/2 ounces tequila

2 ounces bottled clam juice

1 to 2 tablespoons thin salsa or picante sauce

1/2 ounce fresh lime juice

In a shaker without ice, combine the V-8, tequila, clam juice, salsa, and lime juice. Shake to blend. Fill a tall glass three-quarters full with ice. Pour (don't strain) the cocktail over the ice. Serve immediately.

TEQUILA TIP A drink is only as good as its major ingredient. Tomato juices vary. Buy the freshest-tasting, thickest, least salty juice you can find.

TEQUILA COSMOPOLITAN

MAKES 1 COCKTAIL

hottest new drinks of the current cocktail resurgence
sophisticated Cosmopolitan. Usually made with
enough Margarita similarities to have me experi-
with the tequila bottle. Naturally I think the results are
an improvement; so will you.

> 1 ½ ounces tequila
> 1 ounce Triple Sec
> 1 ounce fresh lime juice
> 1 ounce cranberry juice cocktail
> 1 lime wedge

In a shaker half-filled with ice, combine the tequila, Triple Sec,
lime juice, and cranberry juice. Shake well. Strain into a stemmed
cocktail glass, squeeze the lime wedge into the drink, and discard
the wedge. Serve immediately.

See photo on page 48.

EL TORO BLANCO

One of the world's great after-dinner drinks is the Brave Bull:
Pour together over ice in an old-fashioned glass about 2 ounces
gold tequila and 1 ounce Kahlúa; stir well and serve. This is a
variation on that theme, with a touch of heavy cream mellowing
the intensity to create something a little smoother but still
powerful. This drink is a real treat—better than all but the best
dessert on the menu.

> 1½ ounces best-quality tequila, preferably gold
> 1½ ounces Kahlúa
> 1 ounce heavy cream

In a shaker half-filled with ice, combine the tequila, Kahlúa, and
cream. Shake well. Strain into a stemmed cocktail glass. Serve
immediately.

SALSAS, TAPAS

Boilermaker Bean Dip

&

LITTLE MEALS

CHARRED TOMATO
SALSA BORRACHO

MAKES ABOUT 2 CUPS

Tequila adds its usual **je ne sais quoi** to this robust red salsa, aided and abetted by the charred tomatoes. Their sweet depth of flavor comes from the caramelization process they undergo when broiled; the charred peels are pureed right into the salsa. Adjust the heat level to suit your palate, omit the cilantro if you prefer, and serve the salsa with freshly fried corn tortilla chips. Leftovers make a great marinade for chicken (see my Grilled Chicken Tortas on page 99).

> 3 large ripe tomatoes (1 1/2 pounds total)
> 1/3 cup minced white onion
> 4 cloves garlic, coarsely chopped
> 1/4 cup tequila
> 3 tablespoons lime juice
> 1 to 1 1/2 fresh jalapeño chiles, stemmed and coarsely chopped
> 3/4 teaspoon salt, or to taste
> 1/3 cup minced cilantro

Position a rack about 6 inches from the broiler and preheat. (You may also do this on a grill.) In a shallow broiler-proof pan, char the tomatoes, turning them once, until well blackened and soft, about 20 minutes total. Cool. Core the tomatoes, but do not peel, and coarsely chop.

In a food processor, combine the tomatoes, any of their juices, the onion, garlic, tequila, lime juice, jalapeño and salt. Process until fairly smooth. Add additional salt to taste. The salsa can be prepared to this point 1 day ahead and refrigerated.

Stir in the cilantro just before serving.

SALSA BORRACHO VERDE

MAKES ABOUT 2 CUPS

Tart, green, and herbaceous, this salsa is in many ways the flavor opposite of the previous one. In fact, despite the several ingredients in common, you can confidently serve both at the same party, knowing guests will celebrate the contrast between them and happily dig into both. Good on chips, but maybe even better on lighter grilled foods like **quesadillas**, chicken, and seafood.

> 1 pound tomatillos (about 12 medium), husked
> 1/2 cup chopped roasted medium-hot green chiles
>   (see Tip)
> 2 tablespoons tequila
> 1 clove garlic, chopped
> 1/2 teaspoon salt
> 1/3 cup minced red onion
> 3 tablespoons minced cilantro

In a saucepan, cover the tomatillos with cold water. Bring to a boil over medium heat, then simmer until tender, about 10 minutes. Drain, rinse under cold water, and cool.

Carefully core the tomatillos, to preserve their juices, and transfer with any juices to a food processor. Add the chiles, tequila, garlic, and salt and process until fairly smooth. Transfer to a bowl, stir in the onion and cilantro, and add additional salt to taste. Serve within an hour or two.

TEQUILA TIP If you don't have access to frozen chopped roasted chiles, roast 3 large Anaheims in the flame of a gas burner or under a preheated grill, turning occasionally, until lightly but evenly charred all over. Let steam until cool in a paper bag, then rub away the charred peel and stem, seed, and chop the chiles. Canned chopped green chiles can also be used, but you will need to add a fresh jalapeño, stemmed but not seeded, to the food processor to supply the missing heat.

BOILERMAKER BEAN DIP

MAKES 6 TO 8 SERVINGS

I wish I could tell you I had a clear vision of this terrifically tasty dip when I started, then set to work to achieve it, but the truth is, I was just messing around in the kitchen, tossing a little of this and that into a pot of beans. Who knew tequila and beer would add a nutty, yeasty, and completely habit-forming flavor to this good old favorite? The recipe makes a nice, party-sized batch: Mix up a batch of Margaritas too and call some friends.

> One 30-ounce can refried pinto beans ("traditional" flavor with lard preferred)
> 1/3 cup Mexican beer, such as Corona
> 3 tablespoons tequila
> 3 to 4 teaspoons pureed canned chipotle chiles in adobo, to taste
> 2 cups (about 8 ounces) shredded Monterey Jack cheese
> 3 scallions, trimmed and thinly sliced
> Corn tortilla chips, for serving

In a medium, preferably nonstick, pot, combine the beans, beer, tequila, and chipotle puree. Set over medium heat, partially cover, and cook, stirring often, until piping hot, about 7 minutes. Stir in about 1 1/2 cups of the cheese and about three quarters of the scallions and transfer to a heated serving bowl. Sprinkle with the remaining cheese and scallions and serve accompanied by the chips, for dipping.

See photo on page 76.

DRUNKEN FRUIT SALSA

MAKES ABOUT 2 ½ CUPS

Spicy hot and tropically hued (but not really all that sweet), this spirited salsa is great over grilled fish, chicken, or pork.

  1 large sweet red pepper
  1 ¼ cups chopped seeded tomatoes
  1 cup chopped pineapple
  ¾ cup chopped mango
  ⅓ cup chopped red onion
  ⅓ cup minced cilantro
  2 serrano chiles, stemmed and sliced thin into rounds
  2 tablespoons tequila
  1 tablespoon fresh lime juice
  ½ teaspoon salt or to taste

In the open flame of a gas burner or under a preheated broiler, roast the pepper, turning occasionally, until the skin is lightly but evenly charred. Let the pepper steam in a closed paper bag until cool. Rub away the charred peel and stem, seed, and dice the pepper.

In a medium nonreactive bowl, combine the roasted pepper, the tomatoes, pineapple, mango, onion, cilantro, serranos, tequila, lime juice, and salt. Let stand for no more than 30 minutes to blend the flavors. Adjust the seasoning before serving.

MARGARITA-
MARINATED
COCKTAIL OLIVES

These tasty nibbles were inspired by a jar of "Martini olives,"
which came already marinated in vermouth. Why not try the same
flavor-boosting system using the principal ingredients of a
Margarita? Naturally, some chiles also found their way into the
blend. Set out a bowl of these with drinks and watch them disap-
pear!

> 1 cup (about 5½ ounces) drained Kalamata olives, rinsed
> 1 cup (about 5½ ounces) drained garlic- or jalapeño-
>   stuffed green olives
> 12 pickled serrano or jalapeño chiles
> ¼ cup tequila
> ¼ cup fresh lime juice
> 2 tablespoons Triple Sec
> ¼ cup minced cilantro
> 1 teaspoon minced orange zest (colored peel)

In a nonreactive container, combine the black and green olives,
serranos, tequila, lime juice, and Triple Sec. Cover and refrigerate
for at least 24 hours and up to 1 week, stirring occasionally.

To serve, return the olives to room temperature. Stir in the
cilantro and orange zest, transfer the olives, chiles, and marinade
to a bowl, and serve immediately.

TEQUILA-OYSTER SHOOTERS

MAKES 8 SHOOTERS

You'll need at least eight shot glasses to serve these lively snacks-on-the-go (try a restaurant supply house). I say "at least," because in my opinion oyster and tequila lovers can put away a lot of these briny bad boys. Alternatively, designate a shot-glass-washer.

> 8 small oysters
> 4 teaspoons Salsa Borracho (page 78) or any good-quality hot thick prepared salsa
> Hot 'n' Cold Chile Tequila (page 61) or any good-quality tequila, frozen
> 8 lime wedges

Divide the oysters among eight shot glasses. Top each oyster with $1/2$ teaspoon salsa. Fill each shot glass to the brim with tequila. Down a shooter as you would a shot of plain tequila, biting a lime wedge afterward.

TEQUILA TIP These are also great made with clams in place of the oysters.

MEATBALLS IN TANGY TEQUILA SAUCE

MAKES ABOUT 60 MEATBALLS, OR 8 TO 10 SERVINGS

I know I'm at a great party if I've got a highball in one hand and a meatball in the other. This impossibly retro dish is modified (okay, spiced up) from a recipe my mom has made for decades. Serving it won't earn you a phone call from **Gourmet** magazine, but type up the recipe anyway—all your guests will want a copy pronto.

> 2 large eggs
> 1/2 cup minced onions
> 3 cloves garlic, crushed through a press
> 1 tablespoon chili powder
> 3/4 teaspoon salt
> 1 1/4 pounds hot Italian sausage, removed from casings and crumbled
> 3/4 pound lean ground beef
> 2 cups fine fresh bread crumbs
> 1 tablespoon olive oil
> 1/2 cup orange marmalade
> 1/2 cup hot pepper jelly
> 1/2 cup thick and smoky barbecue sauce
> 1/3 cup tequila
> 1 tablespoon fresh lime juice

In a large bowl, whisk the eggs. Add the onions, garlic, chili powder, and salt and stir to blend. Add the sausage, beef, and bread crumbs and mix well with your hands. Shape the meat mixture into 1-inch balls, transferring them to a sheet pan as you go. There should be about 60.

Position a rack in the middle of the oven and preheat to 350°F.

Set a large heavy nonstick skillet over medium heat. When it's hot, add the oil. Working in two or three batches, brown the meatballs all over, about 7 minutes per batch. With a slotted spoon, transfer the browned meatballs to paper towels to drain.

When all the meatballs are browned, transfer to a 9 by 13-inch baking dish. Add the marmalade, pepper jelly, barbecue sauce, tequila, and lime juice, stir, and set the pan in the oven. Bake, stirring often, until the marmalade and jelly have melted into the sauce and the meatballs are just cooked through, about 30 minutes.

Serve from the baking dish or transfer to a chafing dish set over a heating element, if desired. Accompany with toothpicks for spearing.

TEQUILA-CHIPOTLE SHRIMP

The sauce for these hot, sweet, and smoky shrimp goes together from pantry staples, so the dish is a relatively spontaneous pleasure. Serve the shrimp, tapas-like, in a shallow dish with toothpicks for spearing, or provide small corn or flour tortillas and let guests assemble rustic tacos. (The tortillas are also useful for mopping up the deliciously fiery sauce.)

> 2 canned chipotle chiles in adobo
> 3 tablespoons tequila
> 2 tablespoons fresh lime juice
> 1 tablespoon ketchup
> 1 tablespoon adobo sauce from the chipotle can
> 1 clove garlic, chopped
> 2 teaspoons packed light brown sugar
> 1/4 teaspoon salt
> 3/4 pound (about 20) medium shrimp, shelled and
>   deveined
> 1 tablespoon olive oil

In a small food processor, combine the chipotles, tequila, lime juice, ketchup, adobo, garlic, brown sugar, and salt. Process until smooth. Put the shrimp in a nonreactive bowl, pour the mixture over them, and marinate at room temperature for 30 minutes.

Transfer the shrimp to a strainer, letting any excess marinade drip back into the bowl. Reserve the marinade.

Set a heavy skillet over high heat and heat until very hot. Add the oil and swirl to coat the skillet. Add the shrimp and cook, tossing and stirring, until just cooked through but still moist, about 2 minutes. Transfer to a serving dish.

Add the reserved marinade to the pan and bring to a boil, scraping the pan often. Cook for 15 seconds longer. Pour the pan sauce over the shrimp and serve immediately.

TEQUILA TIP Leftover shrimp are rare but possible. Coarsely chop them, mix with any leftover sauce, and use, along with shredded Monterey Jack cheese and sliced scallions, as the filling for a flour-tortilla quesadilla—great with drinks or as the cook's lunch.

SHRIMP "COCTELS"

MAKES 2 SERVINGS

Inspired by those I enjoy on the beach in Mexico, this shrimp cocktail is nothing like the good old American horseradish kind. Spiked with tequila, cilantro, garlic, and jalapeño, it's as refreshing as an ocean breeze and as lively as, well, tequila and Mexico. This is the premium all-shrimp version, although on the waterfront I always order the mixed, which includes clams, oysters, and squid as well. Serve the coctels in tall ice cream soda–type fluted glasses and accompany with saltine crackers, bottled hot sauce, and ice-cold Corona beer.

> 1 pound (about 24) medium shrimp, shelled and deveined
> 1 large ripe tomato (about 10 ounces), cored, seeded, and chopped
> 1/2 cup good-quality tomato juice
> 3 tablespoons tequila
> 1 1/2 tablespoons fresh lime juice
> 1 clove garlic, chopped
> 1/2 teaspoon salt, or to taste
> 1/2 medium avocado, pitted, peeled, and cut into 1/4-inch cubes
> 2 tablespoons diced red onion
> 2 tablespoons diced celery
> 2 tablespoons minced cilantro
> 1 medium fresh jalapeño chile, stemmed and minced almost to a puree

Bring a pot of water to a boil. Add the shrimp and cook, stirring once or twice, until curled, pink, and just cooked through, 3 to 4 minutes. Drain and cool, then cut crosswise in half.

In a blender, combine the tomato, tomato juice, tequila, lime juice, garlic, and salt. Blend with short bursts of power until fairly smooth.

Transfer to a bowl and add the shrimp, avocado, red onion, celery, cilantro, and jalapeño. Let stand 15 minutes to blend the flavors.

Adjust the seasoning. Divide the "coctel" between two tall ice cream soda–type glasses and serve immediately.

GRILLED MARGARITA CHICKEN MORSELS WITH SALSA-SOUR CREAM DIP

MAKES 4 TO 6 SERVINGS AS AN APPETIZER

This mixed bag of savory things—chicken, chips, salsa—is considerably greater than the sum of its parts. (Try the dip on the chicken. Try the chips in the dip. Top a chip with chicken, then add dip, etc., etc.) Creative and communal digging in is the order of the day.

> 2 large boneless, skinless chicken breasts
>   (about 1 1/2 pounds total)
> 1/4 cup fresh lime juice
> 2 tablespoons tequila
> 1 tablespoon Triple Sec
> 1 tablespoon olive oil
> 1 clove garlic, crushed through a press
> 1 cup finely shredded sharp Cheddar cheese
>   (about 4 ounces), at room temperature
> 3/4 cup sour cream
> 1/2 cup hot salsa
> 1 teaspoon chili powder
> Pinch of salt
> 2 tablespoons minced cilantro
> Corn tortilla chips for serving

Split the chicken breasts into halves. Trim them, then cut into 1-inch cubes.

In a nonreactive dish, combine the lime juice, tequila, Triple Sec, olive oil, and garlic. Add the chicken, toss to coat, and marinate for 20 minutes.

Meanwhile, in a medium bowl, stir together the cheese, sour cream, salsa, chili powder, and salt. Let stand at room temperature.

Prepare a medium-hot fire in the grill. Slide the chicken cubes onto flat metal skewers, reserving the marinade. Lay the skewers on the grill rack, cover, and grill for 4 minutes. Baste with half the marinade, turn, cover, and grill for 2 minutes. Baste with the remaining marinade and grill until just cooked through but still juicy, another 2 minutes or so.

Transfer the sauce to a bowl and set at one end of a serving platter. Slide the chicken cubes onto the platter. Sprinkle the cilantro over the chicken and serve immediately, passing the corn chips on the side.

TEQUILA BARBECUE SAUCE

MAKES ABOUT 3 ½ CUPS

and raring to go, this chile- and tequila-spiked sauce
or great grilling. Chicken, ribs, beef, shrimp, sausages—all
ed by a generous mopping of the zippy stuff, both
after. It's homemade, so it's bumpy, but if you must
have your BBQ sauce smooth, just give it a couple of whirls in the
food processor.

> 2 tablespoons olive oil
> ¾ cup minced onions
> 6 cloves garlic, minced
> 2 teaspoons ground cumin
> 2 teaspoons dried oregano, crumbled
> 2 teaspoons crushed red pepper
> 1 teaspoon freshly ground black pepper
> 1 ½ cups canned crushed tomatoes with added puree
> One 14-ounce can mild or hot enchilada sauce
> ⅓ cup tequila
> ⅓ cup fresh lime juice
> ¼ cup honey
> 2 tablespoons molasses
> 2 tablespoons soy sauce
> 2 tablespoons Triple Sec

In a heavy medium pan, warm the olive oil over low heat. Add the
onions, garlic, cumin, oregano, red pepper, and black pepper,
cover, and cook, stirring occasionally, for 10 minutes. Add the
tomatoes, enchilada sauce, tequila, lime juice, honey, molasses,
soy sauce, and Triple Sec. Bring to a simmer, then partially cover
and cook, stirring occasionally, until reduced to 3 ½ cups, about
40 minutes.

For best flavor, let the sauce stand, covered, in the refrigerator
overnight before using. Leftover sauce can be frozen for up to
1 month.

HOT BBQ
CHICKEN WINGS

MAKES 4 TO 6 SERVINGS AS AN APPETIZER

In my house, party food needs to be solid, spicy, and recogniz-
able. These wild wings are exactly that. They make everyone
happy (except for my wife, who has to round up the chicken
bones from the potted plants the next day), and nobody can
stop with just one. Buy chicken "drumettes" if you can—they're
meatier.

> 3 pounds (about 24) chicken wing drumettes, trimmed if
> necessary
> 1 recipe Tequila Barbecue Sauce (page 96)
> Salt

In a large nonreactive bowl, combine the chicken wings and 1 cup
of the barbecue sauce. Reserve the remaining sauce. Cover and
marinate for 1 hour.

Prepare a medium-hot fire in the grill or heat a stove-top grill pan.

Working quickly, arrange the wings on the grill rack or pan, in
batches if necessary, spacing them to avoid crowding. Grill for 5
minutes. Brush generously with sauce, starting with what's left in
the bowl, cover, and grill another 5 minutes. Repeat the brushing
with the reserved sauce, turning, and grilling process until the
sauce is used up and the wings are tender, well browned, and
thoroughly glazed. Season with salt to taste, transfer to a platter,
and serve immediately.

TEQUILA TIP No leftover fresh tequila salsa?
Substitute ²/₃ cup prepared salsa mixed with 2 tablespoons tequila.

GRILLED CHICKEN TORTAS

MAKES 2 LARGE SANDWICHES

A *torta* is a kind of Mexican hero/hoagie/grinder. Fairly improvisational, it typically includes refried beans and guacamole along with meats, cheeses, and chiles. Here's my favorite **torta**, featuring chicken breasts marinated in tequila salsa, then grilled. Eat these overstuffed bad boys outside, preferably at a table you can hose off afterward.

> 1 large boneless, skinless chicken breast (about 3/4 pound)
> 3/4 cup Charred Tomato Salsa Borracho (page 78) or
>   Salsa Borracho Verde (page 80)
> Salt
> 1/2 large avocado, pitted and peeled
> 1/3 cup refried beans
> Two 6-inch crusty sandwich rolls or baguette segments,
>   split, excess crumb removed
> 1/2 cup shredded Monterey Jack cheese
> Sliced pickled jalapeños, optional

Split the chicken breast into halves, pound out, and trim. In a nonreactive dish, marinate the chicken in 2/3 cup of the salsa (reserve the rest) for 1 hour.

Prepare a medium-hot fire in the grill.

Lay the chicken breasts on the grill rack and spread with about half the salsa from the dish. Cover and grill for 5 minutes. Turn, spread with the remaining salsa in the dish, and grill until just cooked through but still moist, another 4 to 5 minutes. Transfer to a cutting board and cool slightly, then thinly slice across the grain. Season lightly with salt.

Meanwhile, in a bowl, mash the avocado. Stir in the reserved salsa and season with salt to taste. Heat the beans (for a quantity this small, it's easiest to use the microwave oven).

Spread the hot beans on the bottoms of the rolls. Sprinkle the beans with the cheese. Top the cheese with the chicken. Spread the avocado mixture over the chicken. Scatter the chile slices, if using, over the avocado. Close the sandwiches and serve.

STEAK FAJITA QUESADILLAS WITH SOUR CREAM AND SALSA

MAKES 4 TO 6 SERVINGS AS AN APPETIZER, OR 2 AS A MAIN COURSE

Great, gooey food. Naturally, leftover fajitas can be used, but these are delicious enough to make from scratch. (If you are using leftover fajitas, you will need about 1 cup chopped meat.) Any salsa will work, but the flavor of Salsa Borracho Verde (page 80) is particularly pleasing here.

> 2 thin-cut (¹/₂-inch) boneless New York steaks
>   (about 10 ounces total)
> 2 teaspoons fresh lime juice
> 2 cloves garlic, crushed through a press
> 1 teaspoon tequila
> 2 teaspoons chili powder
> Salt
> Four 10-inch flour tortillas
> ¹/₂ pound thinly sliced jalapeño Jack cheese
> 3 scallions, green and white portions trimmed and thinly
>   sliced
> Nonstick cooking spray
> Sour cream and salsa, for serving

Drizzle the steaks on both sides with the lime juice. Smear the garlic over both sides of the steaks and sprinkle the tequila over them. Cover and let stand at room temperature for 1 hour.

Prepare a medium-hot fire in the grill. Dust the steaks on both sides with the chili powder, patting it so it adheres. Lightly salt the steaks on both sides.

Lay the steaks on the grill rack, cover, and grill, turning once, until well browned but still slightly pink at the center, about 6 minutes total. Remove from the grill and cool.

On a cutting board, chop the steaks into ¼-inch pieces.

To make the quesadilla, lay 1 tortilla on a flat cookie sheet. Arrange one fourth of the cheese slices evenly over the tortilla. Scatter with half the steak and half the scallions. Arrange one third of the remaining cheese over the steak. Top with a second tortilla. Assemble the second quesadilla.

Spray a large heavy skillet lightly with nonstick spray. Set over medium heat. Carefully slide the quesadilla into the skillet. Weight with a small plate, cover the skillet, and cook until the cheese is beginning to melt and the bottom of the quesadilla is brown and crisp, about 3 minutes. Spray the top of the quesadilla lightly with nonstick spray. With a large spatula, carefully turn the quesadilla. Weight it with the plate, cover, and cook until the bottom is crisp and brown, the cheese is fully melted, and the steak is heated through, another 2 to 3 minutes. Transfer to a cutting board. Cut into wedges and serve immediately, accompanied by sour cream and salsa. Cook the second quesadilla.

Margarita Pie

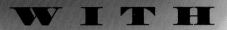

WITH

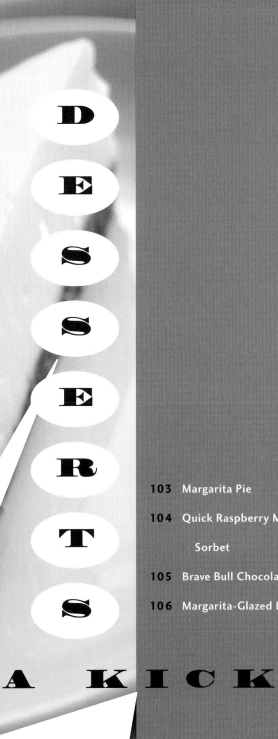

DESSERTS

A KICK

MARGARITA PIE

MAKES ONE 9-INCH PIE, OR 6 TO 8 SERVINGS

Good old Key lime pie gets a real lift from a slug of tequila and a splash of Triple Sec. Since all its ingredients, except the limes, are nonperishable, since I always have limes in the fridge, and since it goes together in minutes, this is the ideal short-notice company's-coming dessert: Toss it in the icebox as the guests drive up and it'll be firm enough to cut by dessert time.

> 4 large egg yolks
> One 14-ounce can sweetened condensed milk
> 1/3 cup fresh lime juice
> 2 tablespoons tequila
> 4 teaspoons minced lime zest (colored peel)
> 1 tablespoon Triple Sec
> One 9-inch (6-ounce) prepared graham cracker pie shell
> Unsweetened whipped cream, for topping
> Thinly sliced lime rounds, as garnish

Position a rack in the middle of the oven and preheat to 350°F.

In a large bowl, whisk together the yolks and condensed milk. Add the lime juice and whisk for 1 minute. Whisk in the tequila, lime zest, and Triple Sec. Pour the mixture into the pie shell. Bake until the filling is lightly but evenly set and the edges of the shell are lightly browned, about 12 minutes. Cool to room temperature, then refrigerate until ready to serve, at least 2 hours.

To serve, cut the pie into wedges and transfer the wedges to dessert plates. Top each wedge with a dollop of whipped cream, garnish with a lime round, and serve immediately.

BRAVE BULL
CHOCOLATE SAUCE

MAKES ABOUT 2 CUPS

I have previously sung the praises of the Brave Bull cocktail (see
my cream-modified version, El Toro Blanco, on page 75) and do
so once again. Here the drink's main ingredients—tequila and
the coffee liqueur Kahlúa—are combined with another of
Mexico's great products, chocolate, to produce a very fine
dessert sauce indeed. Serve it over coffee ice cream, top with
lots of unsweetened whipped cream, and garnish with chocolate-
covered coffee beans. (Or just eat it from a spoon.)

> 1 cup lightly packed confectioners' sugar
> ½ cup (1 stick) unsalted butter
> 4 ounces semisweet chocolate, chopped
> 4 ounces unsweetened (baker's) chocolate, chopped
> ¼ cup tequila
> ¼ cup Kahlúa
> 2 tablespoons heavy cream
> Pinch of salt

In a medium heavy pan, combine the sugar, butter, chocolates,
tequila, Kahlúa, and cream. Set over low heat and cook, stirring
often, until the chocolate is almost melted. Remove from the heat
and continue to stir until smooth. Stir in the salt.

The sauce can be refrigerated for up to 1 month. To use,
rewarm in a heavy pan over low heat, stirring often, or use a
microwave oven.

MARGARITA-GLAZED LOAF CAKE

MAKES ONE 9-INCH CAKE, OR 6 TO 8 SERVINGS

Just a hint of Margarita flavor is all it takes to make this easy cake head-and-shoulders above than the usual teatime sweet. Enjoy it as is, toast it, or use it in place of biscuits in an unusual strawberry shortcake. (Toss a little tequila and Triple Sec into the strawberries too.)

Vegetable shortening for the pan
2 1/4 cups unbleached cake flour
2 teaspoons baking powder
1/2 teaspoon salt
1 1/3 cups sugar
3 tablespoons minced lime zest (colored peel)
6 tablespoons (3/4 stick) unsalted butter, softened
2 large eggs, at room temperature
1 cup buttermilk, at room temperature
1 tablespoon plus 1 teaspoon tequila
1 tablespoon fresh lime juice
2 teaspoons Triple Sec

Coat a 9 by 5-inch loaf pan lightly with shortening. Cut a piece of waxed paper to line the bottom of the pan and press it into place. Lightly coat the waxed paper with shortening.

Sift the flour, baking powder, and salt together twice onto a piece of waxed paper.

In a large bowl, mash together 1 cup of the sugar with 2 table-spoons of the lime zest until moist and fragrant. Add the butter and beat until smooth. One at a time, beat in the eggs. By halves, alternately add the flour mixture and the buttermilk to the creamed mixture; do not overmix.

Pour the batter into the prepared pan. Bake until a tester inserted into the middle of the cake comes out almost clean, about 50 minutes. Cool the cake in the pan on a rack for 15 minutes.

CONTINUED

Position the rack about 6 inches from the heat source and pre-heat the broiler.

In a small bowl, stir together the remaining ⅓ cup sugar, the tequila, lime juice, remaining 1 tablespoon lime zest, and Triple Sec.

Remove the cake from the pan and peel off the waxed paper. Set the cake upright on a broiler-proof pan. Gradually spoon the tequila mixture over the top of the loaf, allowing it to absorb as much of the glaze as possible. Set the cake under the broiler and broil until the top is bubbling and lightly browned, 30 seconds to 1 minute.

Transfer to a rack and cool completely before cutting.

QUICK RASPBERRY MARGARITA SORBET

MAKES ABOUT 2 QUARTS

Using partially thawed freezer staples that require no cooking and churn quickly because they are still so cold, this shockingly pink sorbet is very likely the quickest dessert (aside from a bag of Oreos) that I know of. For a potent—but optional—touch, tequila and Triple Sec are drizzled over each scoop just before serving.

> Two 12-ounce bags unsweetened frozen raspberries, partially thawed
> One 12-ounce container frozen limeade concentrate
> 1¼ cups sugar
> Tequila and Triple Sec, for serving, optional

In a food processor or blender, combine the raspberries, limeade concentrate, and sugar. Process until the mixture is smooth and the sugar is dissolved.

To prepare the recipe without an ice cream maker, just pour the mixture into a glass bowl and freeze.

For a less dense sorbet, churn the raspberry mixture in an ice cream maker, according to the manufacturer's directions. Transfer to a storage container, cover, and freeze until solid.

The sorbet can be prepared up to 3 days in advance.

To serve, soften the sorbet slightly in the refrigerator if necessary. Scoop the sorbet into serving dishes. Drizzle each portion with about 2 teaspoons tequila and 1 teaspoon Triple Sec. Serve immediately.

INDEX